YOUR KNOWLEDGE H/

- We will publish your bachelor's and master's thesis, essays and papers

- Your own eBook and book - sold worldwide in all relevant shops

- Earn money with each sale

Upload your text at www.GRIN.com and publish for free

Bibliographic information published by the German National Library:

The German National Library lists this publication in the National Bibliography; detailed bibliographic data are available on the Internet at http://dnb.dnb.de .

Imprint:

Copyright © 2016 GRIN Verlag
Print and binding: Books on Demand GmbH, Norderstedt Germany
ISBN: 9783668640696

This book at GRIN:

https://www.grin.com/document/412741

Sourav Das

Joyce and the Irish Stagnation

A Journey To Persia and Back

GRIN Verlag

GRIN - Your knowledge has value

Since its foundation in 1998, GRIN has specialized in publishing academic texts by students, college teachers and other academics as e-book and printed book. The website www.grin.com is an ideal platform for presenting term papers, final papers, scientific essays, dissertations and specialist books.

Visit us on the internet:

http://www.grin.com/

http://www.facebook.com/grincom

http://www.twitter.com/grin_com

Joyce and the Irish Stagnation: A Journey To Persia and Back

Abstract

Irish scholarship and writing is very sensitive when it comes to the issue of the of English Colonization, colonial forces, independence and the matter of the Post-Colonial. In fact a very Irish consciousness is present in almost all the prose works, poems and dramas of this nation, and all writers in this trend, directly or by implication have sought to portray these matters through their works. The paper will endeavour to delve into that consciousness of acclaimed Irish writer James Joyce which attempts to create an alternative cultural identity different from the English by orientalising the Irish sensibilities and moulding it as an opposition to English Imperialism. Borrowing heavily from the theories of Edward Said, and from Edward Soja, Bill Ashcroft et al the paper will look to illustrate how Joyce "writes back" to the Empire trying to destabilize the colonial culture; yet his identification with the Orient as a Romantic Refuge contrastively crumbles into a place of degeneration, despair and depravity pinpointing James Joyce the—'The European's'—ambivalence towards the matter of the Orient: as the boy in Araby is made to realise that escapist fascination is a vain attempt. Focussing on the dissolution of Irish Orientalism into English-French Orientalism, I shall attempt to show how Joyce strove to but failed in transforming Dark Rosaleen into a Gaelic Madonna.

Keywords: Orient, Paralysis, Irish Orientalism, Orientatism, Dark Rosaleen

Contents

1. The Irish Situation

On 2nd of February 1882, James Augustine Aloysius Joyce was born to John Stanislaus Joyce and Mary Jane Murray in the Rathgaar suburb of Dublin, a Dublin almost in its 81st year as a part of the greater "United Kingdom of Great Britain and Ireland" as per the Acts of Union 1800 which annexed the Kingdom of Ireland to Great Britain. There have been few corners of the British Empire which have undergone such a complex inter-relationship with England(Britain) than Ireland. Claimed as part of kingdom under the English crown it declared itself a confederacy under the Stuart Kings. Granted partial governance in the 20th century with the passing of the Government of Ireland Act on September 18, 1914 the bicameral Irish Parliament was set up in Dublin with powers to deal most "national" affairs. These carefully selected intricacies in the political scenario problematise Ireland's position when it comes to academia. Ireland's relation with the Post-Colonial can be said to be at best puzzling and complicated. Allowed self-governance to an extent, Ireland could have had afforded to call itself almost independent and this takes away the question of Colony or completely dependant from it. But then again neither could Ireland call itself a self-sufficient power with Imperial England still maintaining a rather firm hold over it, politically and also culturally. Thus hanging somewhere in the middle stood Ireland, its being a confusion, its identity in a limbo. Young James Joyce breathed these winds of confusion as Ireland quite tamely gave in into what the English Imperialists had in store for it. Ireland culturally and politically got defined by its English "oppressors". Paralysis stands as a very important theme in Joycean writing and it is this "culture" or rather the lack of culture that Joyce so famously terms as the "Irish Paralysis". Joyce was no great nationalist but it was his deep desire to overcome this overwhelming sense of numbness that fuelled him throughout his career to attain a remedy for this null in the Irish way of life.

Joyce had famously described Ireland as the 'afterthought of Europe'(Cheng, 1995, p.67)as a centre of paralysis and xenophobic nationalism whose lusty eyed snares the artist must avoid and overcome at all costs if he is to create the uncreated conscience of his race. Throughout his life Joyce strove to attempt the creation of this "conscience"————— a culture which would be "his own" and not be dominated by the popular discourses of the Imperial power watching over it i.e. England and above all be free from its hegemonic social control. Most of his creative endeavours echoed this immense yearning for a space that would be his very own, a space that would usher in an identity which would neutralize that, that was thrown upon him, the Anglican-Irish identity.

1.1 The "Paralysis"

Dublin or for that fact Ireland to Joyce reeked of paralysis, moral paralysis, a city and a country full of people who have trapped themselves in their own mindsets.

'Dubliners strictly speaking, are my countrymen, but I don't care to speak of our "dear dirty Dublin" as they do. Dubliners are the most hopeless, useless and inconsistent race of charlatans I have come across on this island or this continent. This is why the English Parliament is full of the greatest windbags in the world. The Dubliner passes his time gabbing and making rounds in bars or taverns, or cathouses without ever getting "fed up" with the double doses of whiskey and Home rule, and at night when he can hold no more and is swollen up with poison like a toad, he staggers from the side door, and guided by an instinctive desire for stability along the straight line of the houses he goes slithering his backside against all walls and corners. He goes "arising along" as we say in English. There's the Dubliner for you.' (Ellmann, 1983, p.217)

As introduced in "The Sisters" and concluded upon in "The Dead" Joyce used the term "paralysis" to denote a condition of physical and religious torpor which had silently and steadily rendered the Irish existence sterile. He elucidates the dominant theme of despair, resignation and loss resulting from the inevitability of spiritual death, caused by life's experiences in his very first story. It is only after the death of Father Flynn that the boy understands the oppressive religiosity of the Catholic Culture; that the others associate the priest with materialism and decay and in this wake he perceives intuitively in the priest's paralysis the stagnation of his society. His idolised father-figure embodies nothing else but this corrupt society. In articulating the syllables of the word "paralysis" the nameless narrator says that it bore strange resemblance to a 'simony'(buying and selling of spiritual grace) and in identifying the word with an infringement in the Christian doctrine, he unknowingly questions the very persona of the Rev. James Flynn formerly of the Catherine's Church Meath Road. In "An Encounter" the boys cut a dissatisfied figure against the "Father dominated" school-society, but even in their adventure they come across an old man who quite authoritatively gives them advice on books and sex. To their abhorrence and fright he turns out to be a degenerate whose psychological paralysis embodies the sterility of ambition of the Irish society. Similarly stories like "Eveline", "Two Gallants", "After the Race" et al all present the young Irish generation so paralyzed in their will and emotion that they succumb to the past traditions or present conventionalities and end up immobilized.

Spiritual death according to Joyce is defined as 'people who live meaningless lives of inactivity'(Gilbert, 1957, p.55), those he says are the real dead. Joyce had intended his stories to deal with this paralysis when he said 'I call the series Dubliners to betray the soul of that hemiplagia or paralysis which many consider a city'(Ibid, p.55). Consistent among Joycean writing is the yearning to consistently overcome this paralysis. But how does he intend to do so? The state offered no comfort; the Union Jack fluttering over the disbanded Irish House of Parliament on College Green only helped to intensify the subservice. A capitalist and commercialised religion was no provider of faith for the confused, security for the weak or hope for the destitute. "Faith" had been trivialised to the depths of any standard commodity that money could buy. English Imperialism was taking its toll and what was supposed to define the character of a race of people had got subverted into a profit garnering instituti-on. The church stood paralyzed; the schools stood with its masters emulating the English Lords forcing down orders and tenets expected to be followed to the letter. The education system too writhed into a coma. The air that hung over Ireland it would seem carried a po-tent anaesthetic from across the border paralysing the population into rigidity and numbing their senses. The only remedy to this paralysis was the reclamation of the lost native identi-ty, the identity of the Irish people as Irish and not British citizens. And in his attempt at rec-lamation Joyce sought to create a space for himself that would offer him vitality and life against this petrified state of existence.

The majority of the Irish intelligentsia sought refuge in the revival of the "Irish lan-guage" and the Gaelic culture. The Gaelic Revival of the 19th Century intended to re-establish the Hiberno-English[i] through scholars like John O'Donovan, Eugene O'Curry and George Petrie, and the poet and writer George Siegerson. They aspired to revive the latent "Irish Culture" through a resurgence of the language. Another revivalist discipline was the Irish Literary Revival; a brainchild of William Butler Yeats and Lady Gregory it sought to rein-vigorate Ireland's Gaelic heritage through a re-packaging and re-presentation of its folk lores and tales. But with its very inception the latter came under severe attack from the former with the likes of O'Donovan, O'Curry, Petrie and the rest, who denounced it for its works were written in English and not the Irish dialects, and thus tended even more towards Angli-cisation. Eoin MacNeill was particularly scathing when he wrote, 'Let them write for the "English-speaking world" or the "English-speaking race" if they will. But let them not vex our ears by calling their writings Irish and national'(Tierney, 1980, p.66). Patrick Pearse said of the Irish Literary Theatre, recently founded by W. B. Yeats and Lady Gregory, that it should be 'strangled at birth'(Ibid, p.66). Such conflicts stifled the progress of both the organisa-tions and they offered little to almost no realistic respite to the steadily declining Irish situa-tion. Joyce had already given up on the catfight of Irish Nationalism and Nationalist Revival but did favour Yeats and Gregory minutely when in a letter that he sent to his brother Stani-slaus he wrote, 'If the Irish programme did not insist on the Irish language I suppose I could call myself a nationalist. As it is I am content to recognise myself as an exile: and, propheti-cally a repudiated one'(Brown, 2000, xxvi-xxvii). Though Joyce had a steady association with Yeats and Lady Gregory and wrote 'both within and against the moment of the Celtic Reviv-al'(Ehrlich, 1998, p.309) he did not feel fully at peace with this attempt at countering the paralysis numbing Ireland. It became his opinion that no larger groups could rekindle the Irish Identity and Culture which by now he believed was almost beyond repair, and the onus he thought laid with the common population themselves in widening their gaze beyond the remit of the "British" Isles in finding the buoyancy and spirit in a bid to reclaim their lives. Joyce, as we would see through the course of this paper, was questing for a refuge that would help him redefine the Irish civilisation singularly and enable him to reconcile with the prevalent cultural scenario.

2. In looking towards the East

2.1 Irish Orientalism

Irish Orientalism was an intellectual effort on the part of the Irish nationalists to find a connection between the Celts and the Orientals predating the English Imperialism in Ireland. Popularised during the Celtic Revival its aim was to look 'to the East for the highest source of identity and the very origins of the Irish language, alphabet and people'(Ehrlich, 1998, p.309). Irish intellectuals from Samuel Ferguson and Yeats to Lady Gregory, Thomas Moore and James Cousins endeavoured to construct a link between the Celts and the Scythians, variously 'looking to Central Asia, Phoenicia[ii], Egypt or Persia for the roots of their culture'(Bongiovanni,2007, p.29). They attributed the affluent nomadic tribe, the Scythians to have migrated from the Caspian Sea, and moving through Persia, Africa and Spain to have established a colony in Ireland——————— 'the ancient Milesians[iii]....made the epic voyage from Phoenicia via Scythia[iv] and Spain'(Ehrlich, 1998, p.320-321). The Irish populace was their descendent and thus was the bearer of a strong and unique cultural identity different from the English.

Joyce came in touch with the Irish Orientalism through the theosophical programs of the Lady Gregory circle and his fascination for the Orient grew in Trieste, an Austro-Hungarian port on the border between Western and Eastern Europe(Ito, 2009, p.54). Joyce in a lecture in Trieste, citing Charles Vallancey, asserted that the language of the Irish peasants was the same as that of the Phoenicians. Like the Phoenicians it has 'an alphabet of special characters and a history almost three thousand years old'(Ehrlich, 1998, p.322). Joyce even pinpointed the contribution of Scotus Erigena, an Irish philosopher, in introducing Oriental philosophy in Europe through his translation of the eastern texts(Bongiovanni, 2007, p.30).

As a European country appropriated in British subjectivity Ireland was 'an incoherent, shattered and bitter land' having 'neither a literature nor a coherent cultural identity. Sullen hostilities divided the social classes, the political parties, and the social creeds'(Flanagan, 1975, p.44-45). Joyce felt the need of a coherent cultural identity and political freedom from the grip of the English colonial policies and the promise of that came from the myth of the golden Oriental civilization with its 'exotic' and 'satisfying' 'fable of origin'(Shloss, 1998, p.267). Irish Orientalism functioned for him as an 'anti-imperialist strategy' and a reminder of the 'displacement of culture'(Ibid, p.267).

2.2 The "Lush" East

The Orient was, as Peter Barry puts it, 'a fascinating realm of the exotic, the mystical and the seductive'(2002, p.193); a place of romance, exotic being, haunting memories and landscapes, remarkable experiences(Ashcroft et al, 2002, p.24). "Magic" and "Mystery" gets attributed to the "East of snake charmers and fakirs". This intermingling of the magical and mystical into the real gave rise to the "strange" which as an opposite to the "familiar", presented to the European an escape into a space outside the documented lines of restrictive everyday life into a 'pleasant vicious region'(Cheng, 1995, p.81) which functions as the proverbial 'Persia of the mind'(Ibid, p.81). This attitude is captured explicitly in Gustave Flaubert's representation of Egypt; indeed the Orient always catered to the cultural otherness of the West. Flaubert went much beyond the established corpus of knowledge in his expansive and imaginative writing. Orient for him existed as an exotic locale full of mystery and intrigue. It was a place where ancient cultures came to life in the present; a place where Flaubert's imagination could run wild. The Orient acted as the topological playground for Flaubert's creative energies, a place where worldly knowledge met the mind's wildest fantasies and easily blended into a cunning fiction. Flaubert's vision of the Orient was an escape from European restrictions on frivolity.

To Joyce the almost colonized Irishman, an individual who could see his race and people locked up in the proverbial Beckettian paradigm of "nothing happens, nobody comes, nobody goes, it's awful" type of existence, this Orient presented itself as a refuge to the heart parched of life and an identity suffocated by the smog of decadence hanging over it. The lush and exotic Orient offered to Joyce, similarly, an alternative to the stasis that British Imperialism had brought over to Ireland. Frustrated with a government that allowed Ireland to wither away under the British imperialist rule, a church which was too full of corruption to add to a solution, and an academia who did not believe that the Irish could help themselves, Joyce turned to the only escape on offer as he tried to reach out to the great and exuberant East. By applying mystery and romance to it, he attempted to rekindle the charm of life, his life as an Irishman, which was getting lost under the shadows of English commercialism.

2.3 A further Answerable Question

The internet portal Google describes '(To) Romanticize' as '(To) Deal with or describe in an idealized or unrealistic fashion: make (something) seem better or more appealing than it really is'. The action of validating emotion gained in strength as a movement in the late 18th Century; but had existed as long as humans have as man has looked to overcome negativity in life and in his world, and bring forth the soul's desire in order to have a more fulfilling experience of life. In Katherine Mansfield's *Miss Brill* or James Thurber's *The Secret Life of Walter Mitty* both the protagonists represented as lonely contemplative figures, are prone to and romanticize things as they illustrate a vast tendency to reject their own realities and present themselves in their natural equivalence through the way they romanticize what surrounds them. In writing poems like "Death by a Wolf", "The Lake" or "Tomorrow at Dawn" what Alfred de Vigny, Alphonse de Lamartine and Victor Hugo were ascribing to do, was to construct a more agreeable way of existence out of melancholic subjects and decadent nature by fusing into it a strange and forbidden beauty. Industrialisation resulted in a very rigid, commercialised and rational(i.e. dealing with exactly what is there in hand; negation of speculation and what might have been) mode of existence which offered very little refuge and comfort. In a bid to revitalise such redundancy and to overcome the poignancy of his Irish existence Joyce was seeking to present a haunting appeal to the prevalent ways of Irish life by fusing into it a mixture of romance and mysticism, the source of which was the Orient. He wanted to rebuild the appeal of the Irish life and culture which went missing under the shadows of British Imperialism.

3. The East-ing of the West

While writing *Dubliners* Joyce had various discomforts in mind——— Dublin's drowsy denizens, whose conscience and consciousness he felt was almost non-existent and believed that it needed arousing, the mess left on the religious grounds in the wake of the rampant corruption that had entered into the Catholic religion, the Irish intellectuals whom Joyce felt followed Milton and Shakespeare to impress their oppressors and finally the British themselves. Joyce deeply resented that England had let a patronizing Anglo-Irish Protestant oligarchy dominate Ireland and knew that colonial power ——— whatever their stated intention about bringing progress and enlightenment to the colonized people——— dedicated their energies to maintaining power(Schwarz, 2005, p.129). In the exposition of the stories we find a dreary description of the Irish life and lifestyle. Joyce uses a string of negative words------- blind, quiet, uninhabited, detached, useless, wild, feeble, silent et al——— to describe his surroundings. In this 'sombre' 'brown' 'imperturbable' universe the streets are mostly 'silent', the lanes are 'blind' 'muddy' and 'dark', gardens are 'dark dripping'. The leaves of the books are 'yellow', the bicycle pump 'rusty', the priest 'dead'. The air is 'musty' and it hangs over a sterile surrounding. Nature is grave and gloomy with a dusky twilight and the air is stinging cold. This is the common picture of Ireland that Joyce portrays. In his letter to Constantine Curran Joyce writes

> '...I am writing a series of epicleti-ten-for a paper. I have written one. I call the series Dubliners to betray the soul of the hemiplagia or paralysis which many consider a city...'(Beja, 1994, p.35)

He asserts that he was writing the 'moral history of Ireland' and Dublin to him seemed to be the 'centre of paralysis'(Ibid, p.38). Joyce's fear of paralysis comes to the fore in the very first page of *Dubliner* when in "The Sisters", the boy says, 'I said softly to myself the word paralysis(...)But now it sounded to me like the name of some maleficent and sinful being'(D,1). Finding out a pathological unity in *Dubliners* relates to the time when Joyce started writing these stories; he was a medical student then. He diagnosed the embittered restricted life of Ireland as hemiplegia, a partial paralysis. Dublin resembled a city, defeated and degenerate, a city of bleakness, distress and depression with the stench of corruption hanging over it. Politics was a hopeless show, religion was simply a net to trap the spirit of those born in Ireland(Corrington, 1969, p.14). This prosaic setting had hindered the growth of a smooth and optimistic way of life. Joyce felt trapped in a country with an imperial yoke along with his generation. The echoed shouts of the boys in the blind atmosphere in "Araby" is but an attempt to remain animate inspite of the threat posed by the uncle, a symbol of the grave, overbearing authority————— a metaphor almost for Joyce and the Irish scenario.

3.1 Fusing the East into the West

Edward Soja defines Thirdspace as a space where 'everything comes together...subjectivity and objectivity, the abstract and the concrete, the real and the imagined, the knowable and the unimaginable, the repetitive and differential, structure and agency, mind and body, consciousness and the unconscious, the discipline and the transdisciplinary, everyday life and unending history'(Soja, 1996, p.57). *Dubliners* acts as such a space where the two perspectives————— the realist and the romantic; two languages————— the literal and the metaphorical; the reason and the passion, the vertical value-oriented life and the horizontal time-oriented life(Schwarz, 2005, p.136) merge. The stories open with words and phrases which become associated with the culture that is stifling the growth of the Joycean heroes————— 'paralysis', 'blind', 'musty', 'littered', 'useless, 'enclosed', 'fragile', 'grey' and so on————— the real, the literal, the physical space. Joyce attempts to counteract this with an 'idea of escape eastwards' as suggested by Brewster Ghiselin in his pioneering essay "The Unity of Dubliners".

> 'As I walked along in the sun I remembered old Cotter's words and tried to remember what had happened afterwards in the dream. I remembered that I had noticed long velvet curtains and a swinging lamp of antique fashion. I felt I had been very far away, in some land where the customs were strange————— in Persia, I thought....But I could not remember the end of the dream.'(*Dubliners*, 6)

We see the boy here fusing the "strange" and "antiquated" East into his everyday life, especially into the recollection of certain events which we know are not overly dear to him. Firstly, we know that he had resented every word that old Cotter had said; and secondly we see him ruminating about the "dream". We know that when it had first appeared to him, the dream had scared him and he had tried to forget it by drawing up his blanket over his face and think of Christmas. But in this passage with the Orient infused into it he rather willingly seeks out the ending of that very dream. There's a strange sense of romance associated with the recollection, a confused adoration. Persia had given him a strange strength to overcome 'the heavy grey face of the paralytic'.

9

The "far country" reached by the boy in "The Sisters" and sought by the boy in "Araby" are perhaps the same. In walking the streets of Dublin the boy dreams of being in an Eastern land, which he thinks, not very confidently though, as Persia. He goes to the Bazaar bearing the magical name Araby, a word casting an "Eastern Enchantment". The far country as Ghiselin asserts is probably the same with the fabulous Arabia, which is associated with the "Phoenix", a symbol of renewal of life. The boy's response to the name of Araby and his journey eastwards across the city define his spiritual orientation(Beja, 1994, p.112). In *A Portrait of the Artist as a Young Man* adolescence brings in Stephen the desire for the illicit and the mysterious, something which Harry Levin in his ingenious 1951 essay "The Artist" calls as 'something apart from the common walks of life'(Ibid, p.94). His enthusiasm of Lord Byron———— "heretic and immortal"———— does not go well with his classmates. His English masters mark his essay as sacrilegious and he takes rueful consolation in the self-conscious part of the Byronic hero(Ibid, p.94). Joyce's earliest oriental influences must have been from the poetry of Byron itself; his poem, "Beppo" speaks clearly of the Syrian and Assyrian tales. We have already seen how Stephen questions the Jesuit faith and ends up repudiating the Catholic religion. These through the figure of Stephen Dedalus are but Joyce's own attitude towards society and towards himself. As we see, contemporary society rejects the "Romance of Life"; suppressed by the British weight the prevalent Irish culture had become crude and one dimensional. Joyce looked to add that missing dimension to it through the Eastward journey and thus creating out of this fusion a new identity which would stand as an alternative to the "Anglophonic" Irish culture———— Edward Said affirms in *Culture and Imperialism* that we find our identity situated 'between domains, between forms, between homes and between languages'(Said, 1994, p.332). In the syncretisation[v] of the Orient into the drab daily Irish existence, Joyce was looking to rework the Irish culture into something potent enough to act as the prognosis to the hemiplegiatic condition of Ireland. Joyce here looks to bring together the physical and the metaphorical, the muted and the romantic and fuse them into one to give birth to a Third entity, a Third culture, a hybrid which stands opposite to the former and in close association to the latter.

There is a strange deification of the woman in "Araby" as Joyce unpacks the medieval-Christian othering of woman as the mysterious virgin, the Madonna, but within the trope of the Orient. Equally striking again is his description of the "romantic idolisation" of his female characters and of the 'chivalrous idea' as something one bears over the accidents of lust and faithlessness and weariness. He, employing 'an Oriental version of the Holy Grail Quest'(Ito, 2008, p.56) imagines himself as an Arabian Nights hero on a quest to save his princess from the clutches of the evil sorcerer; and to do this he has to cross countless perilous labyrinths and remote areas of unfathomable dangers embodied through the "bargaining woman", "shrill litanies of shop boys" and all the other hustling and jostling. He fuses 'ancient mystery with the sacred legends of courtly love' and it all 'blend(s) together in a contemporary Grail legend...'(Henke, 1986, p.308). A spirit of unruliness diffused itself in him, and under its influence differences of culture and constitution were waived(qtd. *Dubliners*, 11). James Clarence Mangan's poem "Dark Rosaleen" is about a young girl who figures for Ireland herself. Joyce invites us to see Mangan's nameless sister, who is only described as 'brown figure' as a cipher for Ireland in a nationalised extension of feminine othering(Cheng, 1995, p.92). This "chivalrous" idea Joyce gets from the Knights, the Templars, who made their journey eastwards to Jerusalem in search of the Holy Land. Like the Knight protecting his Lady, Joyce endeavours to bear his chalice(Ireland) through the throng of foes(the British Imperialists) in a desired escape from the labyrinth of paralysis and on a pilgrimage for the realisation of the vitality of life.

In *Portrait of the Artist* on which Joyce was working parallely with *Dubliners*, Stephen abandons himself to sensual pleasures. In his encounter with the prostitute he years for both the lover and a mother figure. It is the sensual that Stephen yearns over the sexual. The most resounding example of this is when he spots a girl wading along Dollymount Strand and is immediately struck by her. The girl's sensuality bewitches Stephen. From the young nameless boy to Stephen, to Gabriel in "The Dead" the female characters induce in the Joycean heroes a rapturous ecstasy of chivalric romance and religious adoration. In that epiphanic moment he is overcome by an intense desire to express the beauty in writing——— it is the sensual aspect which appeals to him the most. Joyce has time and again used beauty, mystery and romance to "destabilise" the dominant colonial culture as Harry Levin rightfully documents 'It is like him to lavish romantic sensibilities on an encounter with a prostitute and to reserve his acrid satire for the domain of the church'(Beja, 1994, p.95)— the emphasis here being on the word "romantic". In *Portrait of the Artist* an escape is envisaged in travelling eastward from the city, across the seas to the freedom of the open world(Beja, 1994, p.102)——— an escape from the constricting circumstances of existence under the British rule. In "Araby" the boy clings to the exotic notions of a carnival whose name evokes 'subliminal images of camels and caravans, sheikhs and dark skinned heroes'(Henke, 1986, p.308).

The Orient infused new romanticized Irish culture casts an "Eastern Enchantment" over the soul which gives a heavenly happiness and a direction to life bypassing the hypnotic silence which prevailed under the British subjugation.

3.2 The Irish Orientalist link

Suzette Henke asserts ' In Dubliners the Orient functions largely as an image of alterity—— a symbolic escape from the nets of paralysis associated with Ireland , western Europe, and the heathen "West Country" beyond the pale of Anglo-Irish sophistication'(1986, p. 308). Lynne Bongiovanni in her "Turbaned faces going by: James Joyce and Irish Orientalism" notifies Joyce's genuine fascination of the Orient(2007, p.31-37) and implies that his "falling-in-love" and "romantic idolisation" are in character with the "Irish Orientalism" tendencies which sketched the exotic, magical, mysterious and romantically sensuous East as a cultural forefather to the Irish race. To Joycean characters Orientalist philosophies are a solace and a refuge due to its myth of Irish genealogy which provided Ireland a history very much different from the overbearing colonial history given by England. They find a glimpse of freedom from the stagnant socio-political condition through the romanticized and orientalised images of Ireland, its people and its culture.

4. "Orientalism": The project of Edward Said

"Orientalism" is 'that semi-mythical construct'(Shands, 2008, p.5) originating in the late 18th Century operating in the service of the West's hegemony over the East, primarily by producing the East discursively as the West's inferior "Other". It does this principally by distinguishing and essentialising the identities of the East and the West through a dichotomising system of representation embodied in the regime of stereotypes.

'Orientalism as a western style for dominating, restructuring and having authority over the Orient'(Said, 2001, p.3) conceives the divine and civilisational mandate(Kaul, 2009, p.7) to produce 'the Orient politically, sociologically, militarily, ideologically, scientifically and imaginatively in the Post-Enlightenment era'(Said, 2001, p.3), prime emphasis in our context being on the word "imaginatively". The East was then characteristically produced in the "Orientalist" discourse as variously——— voiceless, female, despotic, irrational and backward over and against the masculinity, democracy, morality, rationality of the West; a domain to be explored and dominated. The Orient existed in the gendering stereotype of the mind and body and offered the "transcendental" European mind a locale of release and perversion. The racialised Orient thus becomes a culturally constructed repository of what might be termed 'Europe's collective daydream', 'the Occidental self's drive for difference, mystery and subversion'(Cheng, 1995, p. 78). A feminised, inscrutable East with its essentialised ideas of aberrant mentality caters to that Id of the European psyche looking for a release and perversion, and the Victorian discourse of Orientalism acts as the Ego rationalising the Id's drive for its bodily needs, desires and impulses.

Since Napoleon's triumph over Egypt the account of the wealth, riches and luxury of the East had got a centerstage in the accounts and memoirs of the western writers; it became a place "where" dreams come true. As Suvir Kaul asserts, the complex world pictures cataloguing the landscapes, people, goods, produces, flora, fauna, fruit, flowers, minerals, metals etc elements which all add to the building of its aura as exotic and alluring(2009, p.72). With time the Orient figured as a holiday resort to the European, fulfilling its drive for the unsaid and unmentionable. With its '...slender tremulous scream of Algerian dancing girls; the female abdomen executing such feats as never before...a laughing, languishing, roguish glance from a pair of Oriental eyes'(Cheng, 1995, p.95) the Orient got embedded in a very pornotropic locale on the sovereign Western consciousness(Said, 2001, p. 8). The only con-notation it now got associated with was a strong sense of promiscuity. For the Victorian the most important role of the East in popular Imagination was a locale of sexual license and perversion within a context of sensual wealth(Cheng, 1995, p.95)———— the original arena of Luxe, Calme et Volupté[vi]. In his epoch making study *Orientalism* Edward Said deconstructs Gustave Flaubert's picture of Egypt(we have already seen the tropes within which Flaubert's representations work) by studying his account of the Ghawazee dancer Kuchuk Hanem. Flaubert's vision of the Orient was, characteristically "corporeal" according to Said, an es-cape from the European restrictions on morality the body and sexuality. Said further states that 'when the Orient appears significantly in the English literature of the early Victorian period it is usually as something eccentric and outré, never as important and central to the organized European culture'(Said, 1983, p.270). In *The World, the Text, and the Critic* Said gives the example of Thackeray, Arnold and even Joyce's childhood favourite Byron speaking of the Orient 'particularly with immaturity and a shoddy lack of urbanity'(Ibid, p.271-72). The lush East was the distant land of untold wealth and unimaginable bodily entertainments of the 'Thousand and One Nights', of Scheherazade, the *Rubaiyat* and of the harems and the houris. Said in *Orientalism* sums up the popular Victorian characterisation of the East aptly in one sentence------- 'The Orient was almost a European invention, and had been since an-tiquity a place of romance, exotic beings, haunting memories and landscapes, remarkable experiences'(2001, p.1); a living tableau of queerness(Ibid, p.103).

5. The Fall of the East

Within the discipline of Irish Orientalism Joyce looked at the Orient as a Romantic Ref-uge. He chose to dwell in the trope of Oriental sensuality and romance———— the 'sensual wealth'————— while ignoring the crude sexuality associated with it. In ignor-ing/suppressing this sexuality Joyce associates a religiosity to his quest that validates his 'confused adoration', as the boy 'bears his chalice through a throng of foes'. Again this relig-iosity authenticated Joyce's tendency of Orientalising the Irish sensibilities as it made Joyce think that he, by creating and developing this space as an opposite to the English, could free "Dark Rosaleen" from their bondage and reinstate her as a Gaelic Madonna. But the fact that the Orient was not an opposite but a binary———— an unequal opposite———— is some-thing that the neither Joyce nor the Irish Orientalists could not, or rather "did not" compre-hend. The "Orient" was a very British and partly French construct aimed at showcasing the latter's superiority over what they deemed to be subservient and any solace acquired through the internalization of the inferior side of the binary, would inevitably fall through.

From the very beginning of his "confused adoration" the boy in "Araby" seems to be absorbed in the rosy ideas about love. He, netted in paralyzed Dublin, wants to change his condition by internalising within himself that 'fabulous Arabia, associated with the Phoenix, a symbol of renewal of life...'(Beja, 1994, p.112). But on arriving at the Araby bazaar all such notions of romance come crashing down. The boy instead of finding a noisy bustling fair full of festivities is confronted with a dark almost secluded "weary looking"(just like Dublin itself) the greater part of which was bathed in darkness. It is in this stark disappointment that the Romance breaks down, and the disappointment is turned into despair when he encounters the salesgirl, in a stall of 'porcelain vases and flowered tea-sets' locked in a mild altercation about something with a couple of Englishmen in a voice that had quietly sexual overtones. The fact that Araby was in fact an English production now dawned upon him. Luther Luedtke had commented on the popular commercialisation and the material commodification of the exotic Orient. This stands as consistent with the boy's epiphany at the end of "Araby" —————'each Oriental rapture ends, characteristically, with the clink of coins and the price of admission'(Cheng, 1995, p.96). The journey of the boy/Joyce to the temple where Dark Rosaleen would be rechristened as the Gaelic Madonna is in fact turned into a journey to the "fleshpots of Egypt" where 'the muezzin's call in the temple is (in fact) revealed to be the enchanting siren song of a harem or a houri'(Ibid, p.95).

The temple of the exotic turns out to be a cheap marketplace presided over by the English oppressors. The "Romantic Refuge" has completely been destroyed and the reality shone so alarmingly bright that it almost burned the eyes of the boy/Joyce.

'Gazing up into the darkness I saw myself as a creature driven and derided by vanity; and my eyes burned with anger and anguish'(*Dubliners*,28)

Indeed his eyes burned with anguish and anger as he realised that the 'pleasant vicious region' of one's Desire are in fact tropes for Ireland's relationship to England. The 'pleasant vicious region' already exists in another dimension———— a debased and colonised Ireland, Dark Rosaleen is not a Gealic Madonna but a cheap flirt selling her wares and her self for the coins of strangers(Cheng, 1995, p.100) and all that Joyce's Orientalist leanings did was to prostitute it even more in a locale of sexual license and perversion where the sensual has no apparent significance.

The boy substitutes the salesgirl with Mangan's sister now. Gary Dyer fittingly observes that the boy who 'associates the girl with the romance of the bazaar and the sacredness of the church' paradoxically 'seems to believe that the young woman in the bazaar reflects badly on Mangan's sister(1991, p.26-27), 'exchanging one distorted image of the female body with another———— the "virgin" and the "whore"...'(Conboy, 1991, p.409). The imaginative world fuelled by Irish Orientalism is corrupted with commercialism, materialism, and sexual impropriety———— the tropes of the functioning of the Orient in Victorian imagination and discourse.

6. The Ambivalence

Joyce had looked towards the East in an attempt to revitalise his failing identity by associating it with the great empire of the Turks, the magic, the mystery, the romance and the beauty. Beauty, mystery and romance have always been considered as elements beyond the physical plane; as something elevated. And by adding it to the Irish existence Joyce was endeavouring to liven the canvas up and elevate it from the position of sterility which British snobbery and commercialism had rendered to it. But as we see his quest for ideal beauty and romance is subverted into a journey to the dark unmentionable quarters where basic and crude sexual pleasures are prioritized. Joyce's refuge for regeneration i.e. Irish Orientalism seeps into the paradigm of the English and French discourse of the Orient. Gazing up into the darkness of Araby Joyce stands chastised as he realises the futility of his quest. In looking beyond the Isles he realised what he is bargaining for is not a "Romantic Refuge" but a "Pleasures Escape" which like all worldly matters is prone to decay and eventually degenerates into despair and depravity. Lynne Bongiovanni in her "James Joyce and Irish Orientalism" affirms:

> The representation of the Orient in Joyce's fiction do little to reconcile his educated sophistication with his endorsement of the widely discredited theories of Celticism that located Irish language and culture in the Orient. In fact, Joyce's depiction of the Orient appears even more conflicted, as he seems at times aware of his country's and his own objectification of Eastern culture, but at other times blatantly reproduces racial stereotypes of the Oriental other...In *Ulysses* just moments before his reverie about the almost magical land of "silvered powdered olive trees", Bloom suddenly changes and is gripped by the impression of a "dead sea in a dead land" that bears no fruit at all, "the grey sunken cunt of the world"(2007, p.31-33)

Joyce recognises his Oriental leanings as an escapist fascination and realises that to "write back" and destabilize the "Colonial" culture he must do it from within the paradigms of that Anglicised culture, which we see in none other than his epic creation '*Ulysses*' where he incorporates and simultaneously abrogates the high and grave epic framework which the English literatures have always held in such high esteem. The English had developed a privileged academic enterprise in the nineteenth century with the classical forms at the heart of that enterprise. In '*Ulysses*' we see Joyce completely giving up his Oriental/"looking beyond" leanings and appropriating the Classical discourse while concurrently parodying the great Homeric framework by building it up with the accounts of daily Dublin life which by the Classical standards is trivial and unworthy to be presented as an Epic.

A great ambivalence towards the Orient could now be seen in the wisened Joyce. Seamus Deane in his introduction to the 1992 edition of *A Portrait of the Artist as a Young Man* says:

Joyce was unforgiving in his analysis of the Irish version of degeneration...the morbidity of his community's condition was...the consequence of...its adherence to the deforming system of beliefs and modes of behaviour that kept the Irish in bondage...the conventional systems by which the Irish lived were borrowed, from both London and Rome; and even their revival was fake, both because it found its ratification in a misty and suspect past rather in the present and because it reproduced--- in its valorisation of manliness, sexual purity, the glory of defeat, the imaginative destiny of the Celts or Gael, the spiritual and religious character of the race—— the very features of colonial-Catholic oppression that it was trying to ease.(IX)

————It makes clear that after *Dubliners* and the first parts of *Portrait* Joyce had no reliance on the excavated history of Oriental lineage. Oriental fantasies, a chastened Joyce assessed, 'threaten to distract the Irish from the reality of their own position in empire and dissuade them from enacting the economic and social changes...'(Bongiovanni, 2007, p.46).

Conclusion

Form the whole discussion we can say thus that Joyce was playing with a "double-vision" of the Orient which in due course of time led to its complete rejection proving Edward Said's maxim that knowledge about the Orient was 'idée recues'(Said, 2001, p.94) and 'collective day-dream'(Ibid, p.52) of Europe. And through his ambivalence towards it, Joyce was prodded into the reality of his very existence. His fusing of the Orient into the Irish life was in fact not any creation of a new and vitalised culture but actually was a latent desire to romanticize the Irish sensibilities to 'make something(the paralysed Irish existence) seem better or more appealing than it really is'—— and we know from our earlier study of the word "romanticize" that one of its major characteristics is "unrealism". Like de Vigny and Hugo what Joyce was looking to do we now know, was to build a more agreeable present out of the melancholic and decadent way of Anglicised Irish existence by adding strange and mysterious beauty to it. But alas this "beauty" was no more than a crude measurement of sexual objectification.

Scope of furthering the Project

From *Dubliners* to *Ulysses* what is consistent in Joycean writing beneath the flashy garbs of modernist creation or stream of consciousness is an attempt to destabilize the hegemonic social and cultural control of the British over Ireland. In this paper I have looked to stay within the boundaries I have constructed for myself and show James Joyce's relationship with the Orient which started with an affinity and ended with ambivalence. But moving beyond this, a Postcolonial evaluation of Joyce and his works as a whole is strikingly possible by cross-referencing his works with the quasi-colonial condition of Ireland and taking into note his persistent experiments in trying to come up with the perfect discipline for the destabilisation———— from looking "beyond" in *Dubliners* to looking "within" in *Ulysses*.

NOTES

[i] From Latin Hibernia, Hiberno-English or Irish-English refers to the o the set of English dialects natively written and spoken in Ireland.

[ii] Phoenicia was an ancient civilization situated on the western, coastal part of the Fertile Crescent and centered on the coastline of what is now Lebanon, Palestine, Israel and Syria. All major Phoenician cities were on the coastline of the Mediterranean.

[iii] In medieval Irish history, the Milesians are the final race to settle in Ireland. They represent the Irish people.

[iv] Scythia was a region of Central Eurasia in classical antiquity, occupied by the Eastern Iranian Scythians.

[v] Termed by Bill Ashcroft, syncretism is 'the process by which previously distinct cultural formations, merge into a single new form'(Ashcroft et al, 2002, p.15).

[vi] 'Luxe, calme et volupté', translated in English as 'Luxury calm and Pleasure' is a 1904 painting by French painter Henri Matisse. The painting takes its title from a line by the nineteenth-century poet Charles Baudelaire and shares the poems subject of an escape to an imaginary, tranquil refuge. The Orient was to the Victorian exactly such a refuge which lay outside the boundary of Western morality. The words Luxury, Calm and Pleasure represent the tropes within which the Orient actually had functioned in popular imagination.

Works Cited

Ashcroft, B. G. (2002). *The Empire Writes Back: Theory and Practice in Post-colonial Literatures.* Hove: Psychology Press.

Barry, P. (2002). *Beginning Theory: an Introduction to Literary and Cultural Theory.* London: Faber and Faber.

Beja, M. (Ed.). (1993). *James Joyce: Dubliners and A Portrait of the Artist as a Young Man.* Hampshire and London: The Macmillan Press Ltd.

Bongiovanni, L. A. (2007, October). *"Turbanned faces going by": James Joyce and Irish Orientalism.* Retrieved 2015, from http://www.ariel.ucalgary.ca/ariel/index.php/ariel/article/download/12/11

Cheng, V. J. (1995). *Joyce, Race, and Empire.* Cambridge: Cambridge University Press.

Conboy, S. C. (1991). *Exhibition and Inhibition: The Body Scene in Dubliners.* Retrieved May 5, 2016, from Twentieth Century Literature: http://www.jstor.org/stable/441654

Corrington, J. W. (1969). *James Joyce's Dubliners: Critical Essay.* (C. Hart, Ed.) London: Faber and Faber.

Dyer, G. R. (1991, September). *The "Vanity Fair" of Nineteenth-Century England: Commerce, Women, and the East in the Ladies' Bazaar.* Retrieved 18 May, 2016, from Nineteenth-Century Literature: http://www.jstor.org/stable/3045191

Ehrlich, H. (1998). *Araby in Context: The 'Splendid Bazaar', Irish Orientalism and James Clarence Mangan.* Retrieved 2016, from James Joyce Quarterley: http://www.jstor.org/stable/25473908

Ellamnn, R. (1982). *James Joyce.* New York: Oxford University Press.

Flanagan, T. (1975). *Yeats, Joyce and matter of Ireland.* Retrieved 2016, from Critical Inquiry: http://www.jstor.org/stable/1342800

Henke, S. (1986). *Journal of Modern Literature.* Retrieved 2016, from James Joyce East and Middle East: Literary Resonances of Judaism, Egyptology, and Indian Myth: https://www.jstor.org/stable/3831497

Ito, E. (2008). *Orienting Orientalism in Ulysses .* Retrieved 2016, from http://p-www.iwate-pu.ac.jp/~acro-ito/Joycean_Essays/U_Orientalism.html

Joyce, J. (2000). *Dubliners.* (T. Brown, Ed.) London: Penguin Books.

Joyce, J. (1990). *Ulysses(1922).* New York: Vintage.

Kaul, S. (2009). *Eighteenth-Century British Literature and Postcolonial Studies.* Edinburgh: Edinburgh University Press.

Said, E. W. (1994). *Culture and Imperialism.* London: Vintage.

Said, E. W. (2001). *Orientalism.* Delhi: Penguin Books India.

Said, E. W. (1983). *The World, The Text and the Critic.* New York: Harvard University Press.

Schwarz, D. R. (2005). *Modern British & Irish Novel 1890-1930.* Malden: Blackwell Publishing.

Shands, K. W. (2008). *Neither East Nor West:From Orientalism to Postcoloniality* . Retrieved May 10, 2016, from https://www.diva-portal.org/smash/get/diva2:212249/FULLTEXT01.pdf

Shloss, C. L. (1998). *Joyce in the Context of Irish Orientalism.* Retrieved May 7, 2016, from James Joyce Quarterly: www.jstor.org/stable/25473905

Soja, E. W. (1996). *Thirdspace.* Malden: Blackwell Publishing.

Tierney, M. (1980). *Eoin MacNeill:Scholar and Man of Action 1867–1945.* Oxford: Clarendon Press.

YOUR KNOWLEDGE HAS VALUE